Red Pandas:

Shy Forest Dwellers

The **My Favorite Animals** *Series*

Claire Johnston

Red Pandas: Shy Forest Dwellers

(The My Favorite Animals Series)

Copyright 2014 Bonnie L. Johnston

Open Clearing Press

ISBN-13: 978-1495942211

ISBN-10: 149594221X

This book is dedicated to
Susan Kendall Johnston,
who made sure
I always had a book to read.

Thanks, Mom!

To thank you for buying this book, I'd like to give you a free e-book.

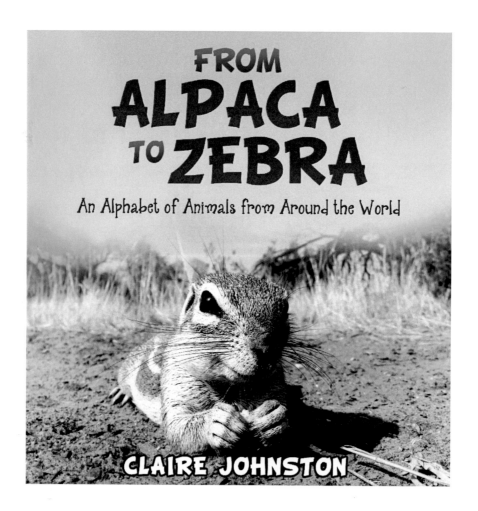

To receive your free e-book, go to:
freebook.authorclairejohnston.com

Table of Contents

What Kind of Animal is a Red Panda?

We used to think that red pandas are a kind of bear or raccoon. But even though they are called pandas, red pandas are not a kind of panda bear. They are not a kind of bear at all.

They are not raccoons, either, but they are related to raccoons. They are also related to skunks, otters, badgers and weasels.

In some parts of Asia, the name for red pandas means "cat-bear."

What Do They Look Like?

Red pandas have reddish-brown fur, like foxes. They also have dark marks around their eyes that look like a mask and long striped tails, like raccoons.

Their stripes help them hide in trees covered with red mosses and white lichens. Their thick fur keeps them warm in the snowy, icy winter.

A red panda is a little bigger than a cat. Red pandas clean their fur by licking it, just like cats do.

Red pandas waddle when they walk, because their front legs are turned inward a little.

Where Do They Live?

Red pandas live in the eastern Himalayan mountains and southwestern China. You can find them in China, Tibet, Nepal, Bhutan, Burma and India.

What Are Their Homes Like?

Red pandas like to live in forests. They spend most of their lives in trees.

Red pandas use their strong paws and sharp claws to climb bamboo stems and hold onto tree branches. A red panda has a special bone in its wrist that pops out to help it climb down tree trunks head-first. This is called the red panda's "false thumb."

Red pandas are territorial. "Territorial" means they choose a place to live, and they do not let other red pandas live with them.

What Sounds Do They Make?

Red pandas are known for making a loud noise: it sounds like they are saying "Wha!"

When a red panda is scared or angry, it makes a noise that sounds like it is part "huff" and part "quack." Huff-quack!

Red pandas also talk to each other by twittering, tweeting, and whistling.

What Do They Eat?

Red pandas love to eat bamboo leaves and shoots. They also eat eggs, insects and small animals like mice.

Red pandas use their front paws to put food in their mouths, like raccoons do.

They are omnivorous, which means "eats everything." In zoos, they have been seen eating birds, flowers, fruit and tree bark.

When Do They Sleep?

When it is cold, a red panda will curl up into a ball and wrap its tail around itself.

Red pandas like to sleep on tree branches or in tree hollows. When it is hot, a red panda may lie on the branch on its stomach and let its legs hang down.

Red pandas are nocturnal. Nocturnal means "active at night." They stay up all night and sleep all day.

What Are Their Families Like?

Red pandas live alone except when they are raising a family. Once she is pregnant, a red panda mother builds nests in hollow trees or in crack in rocks.

Red panda nests are made of twigs, leaves and grass. A red panda may make more than one nest, and move her babies from one nest to the other.

A red panda mother has between one and four babies at a time. Red panda babies are called cubs.

Once her babies are born, the red panda mother feeds them and takes care of them. Red panda fathers do not help take care of the cubs.

When they are three months old, red panda babies start eating food and are able to leave the nest for a short time. They stay with their mother for a year, until their mother's next litter is born.

What Are They Afraid Of?

Red pandas have to watch out for snow leopards, martens and humans.

Snow Leopard

Marten

When red pandas sense danger, they climb tall rocks or trees to get away. If there is nothing to climb, red pandas stand on their back legs so they look bigger, and use their claws to fight.

Red pandas are endangered because people are cutting down more and more of the forests where red pandas live.

Fun Facts: Did You Know?

Master Shifu, the kung fu teacher in the Kung Fu Panda films, is a red panda.

Conclusion

We are learning more about red pandas every day. There are only about 10,000 red pandas left, so many of their forests are protected.

I'm so happy to have shared this information about red pandas with you!

If you and your child enjoyed this book, will you help others find it by leaving a review?

For links to videos of red pandas and information about my other children's books, please visit:

www.authorclairejohnston.com

I look forward to seeing you there!

Claire

Made in the USA
Middletown, DE
23 October 2014